SIMON & SCHUSTER BOOKS FOR YOUNG READERS

An imprint of Simon & Schuster Children's Publishing Division
1230 Avenue of the Americas, New York, New York 10020
Copyright © 2010 by Meghan McCarthy
For information about special discounts for bulk purchases, please contact Simon & Schuster
Special Sales at 1-866-506-1949 or business@simonandschuster.com.
The Simon & Schuster Speakers Bureau can bring authors to your live event. For more information
or to book an event, contact the Simon & Schuster Speakers Bureau at
1-866-248-3049 or visit our website at www.simonspeakers.com.
Book design by Chloë Foglia
The text for this book is set in Paradigm.
The illustrations for this book are rendered in acrylic paint.
Photo of gum vendors and newspaper boys by Lewis Wickes Hine
courtesy of the Library of Congress Prints and Photographs
Division available online at http://loc.gov
Manufactured in China 1109 SCP
2 4 6 8 10 9 7 5 3 1
Library of Congress Cataloging-in-Publication Data
McCarthy, Meghan.
Pop! : the invention of bubble gum / Meghan McCarthy.
p. cm.
"A Paula Wiseman Book."
ISBN: 978-1-4169-7970-8
1. Bubble gum—Juvenile literature. I. Title.
TX799.M33 2010
664'.6—dc22
2008049272

POP!

THE INVENTION OF
BUBBLE GUM

Meghan McCarthy

A PAULA WISEMAN BOOK
SIMON & SCHUSTER BOOKS FOR YOUNG READERS
NEW YORK   LONDON   TORONTO   SYDNEY

On a small street in Philadelphia in the 1920s,
there was a factory owned by the Fleer family. . . .

Inside the factory, lots of gum and candy were made. . . .

Working upstairs was a young accountant named Walter Diemer. His job was to add numbers and balance budgets. He knew lots about math but not much about gum.

There wasn't enough space in the building,
so a new experimental laboratory was moved
into the office next to Walter's.

In came lots of beakers and pots and tubes!
What could be going on?

The big secret was that the company was trying to make a new kind of gum.

Chewing gum had already been around for centuries—men in top hats and women in puffy dresses chewed gum for fun and to cure things like stomachaches.

The Ancient Greeks chewed the sap of the mastic tree.

And American Indians introduced early settlers to

spruce tree resin, a sticky substance that could be chewed.

Ho hum. Gum wasn't *that* exciting. But what if gum chewers could blow bubbles?

Now that would be something—a world full of
bubble gum blowers!

Every day Walter watched what went on inside the laboratory. There wasn't much progress. One day his boss gestured toward one of the kettles containing a gum experiment and said, "Watch that, will you?"

"After a while I was not only watching it, I was doing it," Walter said. He added a bit of this and a bit of that . . . but still nothing. Perhaps making a new gum wasn't possible after all . . . and soon, Walter's boss had given up.

But Walter hadn't. He spent months playing
with different mixtures.

Finally something was happening! Bubbles!
Big, glorious bubbles!

The mixture needed flavor, so Walter added a bit of cinnamon, a dash of wintergreen, a drop of vanilla . . .

Could this bubbling batch be bubble gum?

Walter put a wad into his mouth and began to chew. When the time was right, he blew a magnificent bubble! "I had it!" Walter said.

Excitedly, he passed out the mixture for his coworkers to try.
"We were blowing bubbles and prancing all over the place!"

Sadly, the next day the mixture was as hard as a rock.
"It wouldn't blow a bubble worth a darn."

But Walter didn't give up. Back to work he went!
After many more months of adding this and that . . .
(top secret ingredients he would never share!) Walter found
what he was looking for.

It bubbled and popped. Could this batch finally be bubble gum? To finish off his grand creation, he needed some color. "Pink coloring was the only one I had at hand," said the inventor, so in it went!

A batch was cut into pieces and five pounds of it was brought to a local mom-and-pop store. It was the day after Christmas, and the kids who came into the store got the present of a lifetime! They were the first people in the world to try a bubble gum that worked.

That day Walter gave lessons on how to blow bubbles. Everyone loved bubble gum! "When the kids discovered what it could do, it sold out that afternoon," Walter said.

Walter's Dubble Bubble was such a success
that the Fleer Corporation made
truckloads of delicious bubble gum.

It was delivered to small stores . . .

and big stores alike.

After being promoted to vice president and then later retiring from Fleer, Walter enjoyed the rest of his life in a relaxed manner. He was known to ride around on a giant tricycle, and liked to invite the neighborhood kids over for . . . what else? Gum-blowing contests!

Walter Diemer never got rich from his invention, but he didn't seem to mind. "I've done something with my life," he said. "I've made kids happy around the world."

Not only did Diemer invent something the company had given up on making, but he also helped save the company. The Fleer Corporation, according to Diemer, was failing. "At the Christmas party in 1927, the president told me I probably wouldn't have a job at this time next year because business was so bad." Thanks to Dubble Bubble, it lasted for another seventy years.

Many workers at Fleer were skeptical of Diemer's new invention. He said, "The workers in the mixing room thought that this new stuff was terrible. 'It's too heavy, you're going to break the mixer,' the mixing room supervisor told me. The workers grumbled on in German while the ingredients were mixing."

Diemer spent many happy years at Fleer, both selling and trying new gum. By the time he retired in 1970 he was the senior vice president of the company. And despite all the sugary gum he sampled, he still had all his own teeth, or so he claimed in an interview when Diemer was eighty-five.

After his first wife, Adelaide, died, Diemer remarried at the age of ninety-one. "We're both eccentrics. At least one of us is," he said of his new marriage. He had outlived his first wife, and his son and daughter, and admits "I was down in the dumps," until he found Florence, age seventy-four. Diemer met Florence at a retirement home, which contrasted greatly from the big house located by the ocean he had lived in and had grown to love. As Florence put it, "It's about time he got happy. He's had a pretty gloomy world. He'll be okay from now on." And he was. Walter Diemer lived to the ripe age of ninety-three.

Today 40 million pieces of bubble gum are sold daily. American kids spend about a half billion dollars on gum each year. Everyone loves bubble gum! The next time you blow a big bubble, remember Walter Diemer. You have him to thank.

In the early twentieth century city kids sold chewing gum and newspapers to help support their families.

FACTS ABOUT GUM

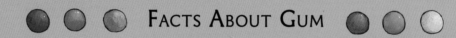

Who chewed the most gum in 2006? If you voted kids, you'd be wrong. The answer is college-educated women in their thirties. Go figure!

Studies have shown that chewing gum actually helps people concentrate.

If you swallow your gum, it won't stay in your stomach for seven years, as folklore suggests. It ends up in the same place the rest of your food does.

Chewing gum on an airplane will prevent your ears from popping. The more chewing you do, the more saliva you make, and the more you will swallow—which causes the pressure in your head to become balanced.

Detectives can find criminals by comparing their chewed gum (an imprint of their teeth is left in it) to their dental records.

If you chew gum nonstop for a year straight you will lose eleven pounds (good luck with that, though!).

Chewing sugarless gum can prevent tooth decay (increasing saliva gets rid of that nasty bacteria, and xylitol found in gum is thought to actually heal cavities).

A new kind of gum is being invented—one that doesn't stick. Professor Cosgrove is a British scientist who works with plastics. After noticing blackened wads of gum on the sidewalks, he thought, "You think perhaps it's pigeon poo." He tested his new invention on some sidewalks in England and found that it rinses off with rainwater.

MORE FACTS ABOUT GUM

Scientists found a wad of chewed birch resin in Sweden that dates back 9,000 years, to what would be considered caveman days.

Dubble Bubble was included in ration kits for American soldiers serving in World War II.

Gum was rationed during World War II because of a shortage of chicle, Siamese jelutong sap, and sugar. Walter Diemer remembered this, saying, "The government took all the materials used in bubble gum. . . . It almost broke my heart."

Desperate times called for desperate measures. During World War II some kids kept their Dubble Bubble "alive" in glasses of water at night. Some even managed to continue chewing one piece for as long as a month!

Dubble Bubble, although harder and not as flavorful as newer brands, does blow some of the best bubbles. It's recommended that you chew the gum until it loses most of its flavoring, or chew a sugarless brand. The sugar in the gum makes it harder to blow big bubbles because it doesn't stretch well.

Susan Montgomery Williams of Fresno, California, is the record holder for the largest bubble—twenty-three inches.

For more than forty-five years, thousands have stuck chewed gum to the walls of buildings along an alley in San Luis Obispo, California. It's unofficially known as "Bubble Gum Alley." Seattle's Post Alley has been collecting gum deposits since the early nineties.

Post Alley in the Pike's Place Market in Seattle

QUOTES IN THE BOOK CAN BE FOUND IN THE FOLLOWING BOOKS AND ARTICLES

"As Exams Loom, Students Find Hope in a 'Stick'; Cornell University Class Tests Benefits of Chewing Gum During Exam." *PR Newswire* (1 November 2007).

Brubaker, Jack. "The Fellow Who Invented Bubble Gum Lives in a Local Retirement Village." *The Scribbler* (13 July 1990): A-10.

"Dubble Bubble Man, Neffsville Resident, 87, Fondly Recalls Inventing Bubble Gum in 1928." *Lancaster New Era* (15 August 1992): A-1.

Foreman, Judy. "Is Chewing Gum Good for You?" *Boston Globe* (17 July 2006): C-2.

Hendrickson, Robert. "A Genius, Gum Inventor Was Smack in the Middle of a Pop Explosion." *Chicago Tribune* (30 August 1990): 1.

Hendrickson, Robert. *The Great American Chewing Gum Book.* Radnor, PA: Chilton Book Company, 1976

"It's New, It's 'Increda Bubble'." *Oakland Post* 471 (19 March 1980): 13.

Joanou, Grace. "His Colors are Red, White, Blue . . . and Pink. This Retired Resident of County Was Bubble Gum Inventor in 1928." *Senior Citizens Intelligencer Journal* (4 February 1991): C-12.

Johnson, Rheta Grimsley. "Inventor's Life was Bursting with Sweet Success." *The Atlanta Journal-Constitution* (19 January 1998): B-2.

Kettle, Martin. "Walter Diemer, Inventor of Bubble Gum, Dies Aged 93." *The Guardian* (13 January 1998): 10.

Kleiner, Carolyn and Mary Brophy Marcus. "In Memoriam." *U.S. News & World Report* 124.3 (26 January 1998): 15.

Rogers, Amanda. "75 Years Ago, a Pink Phenomenon Burst Forth | Bubble Gum Quickly Popped into the Eye of the Public." *The San Diego Union-Tribune* (24 April 2003): E-2.

Tanenbaum, Sharon and Ashley Tate. "Chewing Gum 101." *Real Simple* 9.5 (May 2008): 62.

Tagliabue, John. "Gum That Won't Stick to Shoes? It's in the Works." *New York Times* (26 December 2007): C-3.

"The Invention That Didn't Just Blow Over; Walter Diemer Never Thought His Bubble Gum Would Stick Around." *Philadelphia Inquirer* (23 August 1992): B-2.

Van Ingen, Lori. "Love Bubbles Over at Lancashire." *Intelligencer Journal* (19 September 1996): B-1.

Vargas, Daniel J. "Bubble Gum Leaves Its Mark on History. After 75 Years, We're Still Blown Away by the Childlike Joy of Gum. Well, Maybe Some of Us Aren't." *San Antonio Express-News* (13 Jun 2003): 1-F.

"Walter Diemer, Inventor of Bubble Gum in 1920s." *Chicago Tribune* (13 January 1998): 8.

"Walter Diemer, 93, Bubble Gum Inventor." *Philadelphia Inquirer* (11 January 1998): C-16.

Wittmaier, Bruce C. "Bubble Gum Chewy Stuff Developer Retired to Lancaster County." *Sunday News* (15 July 1990): G1.